in
the
news™

TSUNAMIS

Ann Malaspina

ROSEN
PUBLISHING®

New York

To Paul, who has kayaked the waves in Oahu and climbed the volcanic cliffs of Santorini, and knows the perils of tsunamis

Published in 2007 by The Rosen Publishing Group, Inc.
29 East 21st Street, New York, NY 10010

First Edition

Library of Congress Cataloging-in-Publication Data

Malaspina, Ann, 1957–
Tsunamis / Ann Malaspina.—1st ed.
    p. cm.—(In the news)
Includes bibliographical references and index.
ISBN-13: 978-1-4042-0978-7
ISBN-10: 1-4042-0978-6 (library binding)
1. Tsunamis—Juvenile literature. 2. Indian Ocean Tsunami, 2004—
Juvenile literature. I. Title.
GC221.5.M35 2007
363.34'94—dc22
                                                                2006024436

Manufactured in the United States of America

On the cover: Clockwise, from left: An aerial view from a U.S. Navy helicopter of the damage done to Sumatra, Indonesia, after a deadly earthquake sparked a tsunami in 2004; a woman walks through the destroyed Indian city of Nagapattinam after the same tsunami swept through southern India; and a video still of the flooding in Banda Aceh, Indonesia, following the tsunami's effect there in 2004.

contents

Harbor Wave

Racing across the open ocean at the speed of a commercial jet, a tsunami wave is barely visible. It may raise the ocean's surface only a foot or two, but its appearance doesn't tell the whole story. In fact, a tsunami is generally hundreds of miles wide and as deep as the ocean's floor. One of the most powerful natural forces on Earth, the tsunami pushes tons of water relentlessly forward, building higher as it nears shallow coastlines. Only when it slams into land is the wave's full fury released.

Along the shore, the gigantic wave lifts boulders and coral reefs, and disintegrates beaches. As it floods the land, a tsunami yanks trees by their roots and tears buildings from their foundations. Cars and boats are thrown about like toys, and bridges are crumpled like paper. People are pulled into strong currents. When the wave retreats, the water drags most everything back into the sea.

What Causes Tsunamis?

Tsunamis are not like typical waves at the beach or the battering surf of a hurricane. Tsunami waves are not caused by wind, weather, or high tides. A sudden, violent movement of the ocean floor is the trigger for a tsunami. The disturbance may be caused by an earthquake, volcanic eruption, landslide, or even a fallen meteorite. Tsunamis are sometimes called tidal waves, but this classification is incorrect. Tides move with the gravitational pull of the sun and moon, and do not produce tsunamis. Still, tsunamis that occur at high tide may be more destructive.

Fortunately, tsunamis are rare. Around the world, only about ten tsunamis occur every year, and 100 in a decade. Most tsunamis are small and barely noticeable, doing little damage to coastlines. The water level may rise by only a few inches. Usually, just one major tsunami forms in a

year, but even that number is unpredictable. Three major tsunamis, in Nicaragua, Japan, and Indonesia, happened in less than twelve months in 1992 and 1993.

The Ring of Fire

It is the deadly tsunami that the world notices, when waves as high as 300 feet (91 meters) flow inland, destroying everything in their path. On August 27, 1883, the Krakatoa volcano erupted in the Indian Ocean, spawning four tsunamis that drowned 36,000 people on nearby islands. More than a century later, the Indian Ocean was struck by an even more devastating tsunami. The day after Christmas in 2004, an undersea earthquake near the island of Sumatra generated a series of tsunamis that slammed into fourteen countries, killing more than 250,000 people and leaving millions injured and homeless. Many months later, villages in the region were still not rebuilt and thousands of people remained in tent villages.

> *The day after Christmas in 2004, an undersea earthquake near the island of Sumatra generated a series of tsunamis that slammed into fourteen countries, killing more than 250,000 people . . .*

Tourists flee the ocean off coastal Thailand, moments after the waters receded and seconds before six tsunami waves slammed toward the beach on December 26, 2004, killing thousands.

Residents wade through flooded streets to higher ground moments after a tsunami struck Banda Aceh province, Indonesia, on December 26, 2004.

The word "tsunami" actually comes from two Japanese symbols, *tsu* for "harbor" and *nami* for "wave." Tsunamis are especially dangerous in narrow harbors. When the waves squeeze into smaller spaces, they intensify. Japan, an island nation in the Pacific Ocean, has seen many tsunamis.

In 1896, an earthquake off the coast caused a tsunami near the port city of Sanriku that killed 27,000 people. An earthquake in the Japanese Sea near Hokkaido produced another deadly tsunami on July 12, 1993. Waves swept over the island of Okushiri, leaving about 200 people dead.

Japan is in the part of the world most at risk for tsunamis. Although tsunamis can develop in any water and reach any coastline, most originate in a zone of volcanoes and earthquakes known as the Ring of Fire, circling the Pacific ocean. This area is located where the Pacific plate of the earth's crust collides with surrounding plates. More than 75 percent of the world's volcanoes lie in this unstable Pacific Basin region that stretches from New Zealand, along the edge of Asia, across the Aleutian Islands of Alaska, and down the west coast of North and South America. The states of Hawaii, Alaska, California, Oregon, and Washington lie in the danger zone, and all have seen Pacific tsunamis.

Tsunami Warning Systems

Nothing can stop a tsunami from rolling across the sea, but tsunami warning systems and public education save lives. Tragically, no tsunami warning siren rang on May 22, 1960, when the largest earthquake ever recorded (measuring 9.5 on the Richter scale) shook the Pacific near Chile. The sea rose in the port of Corral in southern Chile. The first wave pulled back, leaving boats perched on the dry harbor before a wall of water consumed the city. The tsunami left more than 2,000 people dead in Chile before it sped across the Pacific to Hawaii and onto Japan. Since that disaster, Pacific region countries have

NORTH AMERICA

ASIA

Aleutian trench

Kurile trench
Japan trench

Ryukyu trench

Izu Bonin trench

Pacific Ocean

Philippine trench

Marianas trench

Ring of Fire

INDONESIA

Bougainville trench

Middle America trench

Java Sunda) trench

AUSTRALIA

Tonga trench

Peru- Chile trench

0   2,000 mi

0   2,000 km

Kermadec trench

NEW ZEALAND

SOUTH AMERICA

The Ring of Fire is an area in the Pacific Basin prone to frequent earth-quakes and volcanic eruptions, activities that can trigger tsunami waves due to displaced ocean water.

worked together to warn people about tsunamis. Today, the International Pacific Tsunami Warning System protects the people of Chile and the entire Pacific Basin. The warning system keeps watch for tsunamis, providing people with the extra minutes necessary to escape. Education is also vital. People on coasts need to know evacuation routes and safety procedures. Even climbing a tree or holding onto a rooftop can save lives during a tsunami.

2

A Great Big Black Wall

I looked out and saw this great big black wall coming in . . . The noise was terrific, the rolling . . . And then you heard the screaming. You look and people were stomping, trying to reach earth, trying to get out . . . Then came the crash . . . Well, it hit buildings, the lighthouse, and the railroad track, and everything . . .
—Kapua Heuer, a survivor of the 1946 tsunami in Hilo, Hawaii

Hawaiians call tsunamis *Kai e'e*, and they have learned to fear and respect them. Survivors will never forget the tsunami that slammed into Hilo, Hawaii, on April 1, 1946. A 7.8 magnitude earthquake in the Aleutian Islands of Alaska triggered the giant waves. The tsunami first crashed into the island of Unimak, demolishing the Scotch Cap Lighthouse on top of a cliff and killing five workers. It then sped 2,300 miles (3,701 kilometers) across the Pacific to the Hawaiian Islands. Nearly five hours later, a wave crashed like a freight train into Hilo. Water flooded the streets, flattened buildings, and left 159 people dead. Just fourteen years later, on May 22, 1960, another deadly tsunami, this one caused by a Chilean earthquake, battered Hilo, killing sixty-one people.

Earthquakes

Unlike regular waves, tsunamis are generated by disturbances on the ocean floor. Regular waves are formed by wind moving over the ocean surface. Friction between the wind and water creates energy, moving the water in circles and producing waves. The waves swell as the wind quickens and die down when the wind slows. In contrast, tsunamis are not affected by wind or tides.

A tsunami is set off by a violent upheaval in the ocean floor, like the Aleutian Islands earthquake or the Krakatoa volcanic eruption. The floor suddenly shifts, displacing huge amounts of water. As the water jolts up and settles back down, the energy is turned into tsunami waves. Undersea earthquakes are the most common trigger of tsunamis. They are caused by tension in the earth's crust, which is made up of moving parts known as tectonic plates. Some plates, like the Pacific plate, are very large. Sitting on top of the earth's softer mantle, the plates drift sideways and up and down, pushing against each other and moving apart. A process called subduction occurs when one plate is pulled beneath another, pushing the second plate upward. The stress builds until it is released in an earthquake. This vertical earthquake, known as a thrust fault earthquake, is the most frequent cause of tsunamis.

After being adrift for thirty hours, fifteen-year-old Yoshikazu Murakami was rescued from the tsunami waves that stormed Hilo, Hawaii, on April 1, 1946.

Landslides

Underwater and coastal landslides also initiate tsunamis. Landslides can be sparked by an earthquake, volcano, or a buildup of rocks that slides into the sea. As debris falls into the water, a tsunami forms, just like during an earthquake. An offshore landslide deep in the Mediterranean Sea produced a tsunami that slammed into Nice, a seaside resort on the coast of France. On October 16, 1979, two tsunami waves hit the coast along a 36-mile (60 km) stretch. The waves overturned boats and about a dozen people drowned.

Although most tsunamis occur in the ocean, land-slides can provoke the waves in small water bodies such as lakes and fjords. A fjord is a long, narrow channel bordered by high walls of rock or ice.

Volcanic Eruptions

Volcanic eruptions in or near the ocean can cause tsunamis, too. Some eruptions spur violent undersea earthquakes and landslides. Pyroclastic flows of hot gasses, volcanic ash and pumice, and other fragments pouring from a volcano into the ocean can generate enough force to create a tsunami. If the large crater formed by the eruption collapses and fills with water, the sudden shift in the ocean can produce the big waves. The most famous eruption in history spurred deadly tsunamis in the Indian Ocean. The Krakatoa volcano lies in the Sunda strait between Sumatra and Java in Indonesia. The volcano had been dormant for more than 1,400 years when people began hearing explosions, seeing smoke and ash, and feeling small earthquakes in 1883. On August 26, and continuing through the next day, Krakatoa erupted four times. The thunderous explosions shook the earth like bombs, and were heard as far away as Australia. Hot smoke, thick with volcanic debris, shot high into the air and the sky blackened.

Pyroclastic flows poured into the sea, generating huge tsunamis. The volcano collapsed into itself, and water rushed into the crater. Witnesses reported four tsunamis during the hours that followed. The giant waves pushed out in all directions from Krakatoa. Swells as high as 120 feet (38 m) fell onto nearby Java and Sumatra. Heavy coral rocks were thrown onto land, and a steamship was lifted and dropped a mile upstream. The waves traveled beyond the Indian Ocean, raising water levels around the world. Thirty hours after the eruption,

The *Illustrated London News* from September 8, 1883, offered illustrations of the August 1883 eruption of the Krakatoa volcano between Sumatra and Java in Indonesia.

the water rose in the English Channel. In Sumatra and Java, the tsunamis killed more than 36,000 people and flattened 126 villages.

Meteorites

Far less likely than volcanic eruptions, a fallen meteorite may also set off a tsunami. Meteorites are objects from space that travel through the atmosphere. Most burn out before landing. Still, scientists predict that if a meteorite landed in the Atlantic Ocean, tsunamis could flood the East Coast of the United States. The chance of this occurring is slight. No meteorite has fallen to Earth in recorded history. However, scientists have found craters that they believe were long ago formed by meteorites such as one near Chicxulub, on Mexico's Yucatan Peninsula. Some scientists believe this meteorite caused worldwide tsunamis and climate changes sixty-five million years ago that led to the extinction of the dinosaurs.

Deadly Force

All tsunamis have common characteristics. The waves begin on the ocean floor and move through the entire water column, packing tremendous power. People compare a tsunami to a rock dropping into a pool of water

People watch off the coast of southern India as a car and other debris are washed away after tsunami waves rocked Tamil Nadu following the Indonesian earthquake of December 2004.

and sending out ripples in all directions, only the ripples are monstrous waves. They move in all directions from the source of energy. In fact, a tsunami is not one wave, but a series of waves. The first wave may not be the largest; often, a tsunami includes three or more waves.

What makes a tsunami so distinctive is its long wave length. A wave length is the distance between the crests, or tops, of succeeding waves. The crests of tsunami waves may be 300 to 400 miles (500–650 km) apart. The waves take from ten minutes to an hour or more to pass any point. Because they are so long, when they hit land, the water keeps coming. While regular waves exist only briefly and travel a few miles or less, tsunamis can last for a full day, speeding thousands of miles before breaking at land. Tsunamis are also very wide and may stretch hundreds of miles across.

Not all tsunamis travel long distances. Local, or nearfield, tsunamis are caused by nearby earthquakes, landslides, or volcanoes. Distant, or farfield, tsunamis move across the ocean many miles from their source. The 9.5 magnitude earthquake that shook Chile in 1960 produced local and distant tsunamis. Within fifteen minutes, big waves hit the Chilean shore. Waves also sped across the Pacific, crashing into Hilo fifteen hours later. Twenty-two hours after the earthquake, the tsunami reached Japan, more than 10,563 miles (17,000 km) from the epicenter. Still, most tsunamis are regional, limited by the size of the earthquake or disturbance, and the shape of the ocean floor.

In the open sea, tsunamis are not very high, only 1 to 2 feet (30–60 cm). People cannot see or feel them because of the long wave length. When the tsunami neared Hilo in 1946, ships at sea did not rise with the waves, even though people onboard could see the tsunami slam into shore moments later. While a tsunami in mid-ocean is barely visible, it is moving fast. The speed of a tsunami depends on the ocean depth. Tsunamis travel about

475 mph (764 km) in 15,000 feet (4,572 m) of water, but only up to 40 mph (64 km) in 100 feet (30 m) of water, according to the National Oceanic and Atmospheric Administration (NOAA). As the wave slows near shore, the water increases and the crest rears higher.

Tsunamis intensify as they near land. As the coastal water gets shallower, the waves build in strength and grow bigger. If a tsunami squeezes into a harbor or bay, its force is focused in shallower water and it becomes deadlier. Tsunamis usually look like very high tides moving swiftly onto shore. Sometimes the tsunami arrives on land as a bore, a wall of water with a steep front. Only rarely does a tsunami look like breaking storm waves. Sometimes, not always, the sea seems to pull away from the shore before a tsunami. This phenomenon, known as *Kai mimiki* in Hawaiian, is caused by a leading depression wave—a wave that leads with its trough, or lowest point. People often rush to see the strange sight, and are soon caught by the tsunami flood.

Sometimes the sea seems to pull away from the shore before a tsunami. This phenomenon, known as Kai mimiki *in Hawaiian, is caused by a leading depression wave. The wave leads with its trough, or lowest point. People often rush out to see the strange sight, and are soon caught by the tsunami flood.*

Tsunamis reach their full height as they slam into shore. Typical wave heights of 10 to 20 feet (3–6 m) during big tsunamis can destroy harbors and buildings. Some tsunamis are even higher. The giant wave that crashed into Okushiri, Japan, in 1993 measured 105 feet (32 m) tall. One of the most extraordinary tsunamis was in Lituya Bay, Alaska, on July 9, 1958. A landslide fell into the bay, generating a tsunami that surged 1,720 feet (524 m) on the opposite shore, higher than the Empire State Building. As the tsunami floods over land, the highest point of the flooding is called the run-up. Major tsunamis can have run-ups of 10 to 50 feet (3–15 m), causing serious flooding problems far inland. The tsunami at Lituya Bay flooded five square miles.

Witnesses report terrifying roars when a tsunami approaches land. As it floods land, wild currents create whirlpools. The tsunami loses energy, but the water is still forceful and dangerous. The tsunami that flooded the coast of Chile in 1960 cut a path of destruction far from shore. The village of Queule, a mile inland, was virtually washed away. Some villagers had fled to high ground during the earthquake, but many people died when the tsunami pushed the local river over its banks. When tsunamis fall back into the ocean, they drag loose objects with them. Cars, slabs of wood, telephone poles, as well as gas and chemicals, are pulled into the ocean. People, too, may be caught in the moving debris.

The Fury of the Waves

3

As the sea was driven back, and its waters flowed away to such an extent that the deep sea bed was laid bare, many kinds of sea creatures could be seen . . . Huge masses of water flowed back when least expected, and now overwhelmed and killed many thousands of people . . . Some great ships were hurled by the fury of the waves onto rooftops, and others were thrown up to two miles from the shore.

—Ammianus Marcellinus

The famous Roman historian Ammianus Marcellinus was describing a tsunami that overwhelmed Alexandria, Egypt, on August 23, AD 365, but his words paint a familiar picture of other tsunamis, both ancient and modern. Slamming into land with awesome energy, the giant waves ravage everything in their paths. Whether a tsunami slams into a beach or surges over a crowded city, the waves flatten landscapes. In fact, powerful tsunamis have altered Earth's geographic and human history.

Cultures Disappear

A volcanic eruption on an island in the Aegean Sea caused a giant tsunami that may have destroyed an entire civilization. The volcano was on the island of Thera, now Santorini, lying between Greece and Turkey. By 1600 BC, the people of Thera were part of the Minoan civilization, a flourishing Bronze Age culture. The center of the Minoan culture was the island of Crete, lying 72 miles (115 km) south of Thera. The Minoans were seamen, traders, architects, and artists. They built elegant temples, painted murals, and wrote in hieroglyphs.

The Minoan civilization could not survive a major disaster, though. Some scientists estimate the volcano erupted between 1650 and 1600 BC, tearing Thera apart and covering the sky in ash and pumice. Thera broke into a group of smaller islands, which today surrounds the volcano's crater. Possibly alerted by earthquakes before the eruption, the Minoans may have fled in time because archaeologists who excavated in Santorini in the 1960s found no human remains. Nevertheless, the eruption generated tsunamis that sped outwards in all directions across the Aegean. The waves reached Crete, overwhelming the harbors and farm fields that people needed to survive. Soon after, the Minoan civilization disappeared.

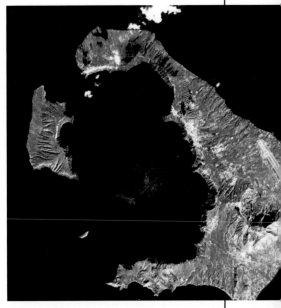

This is a satellite view of Santorini volcano in the Aegean Sea. The eruption of Santorini around 1650 BC was among the largest in the last 10,000 years.

Cities Destroyed

The Atlantic Ocean rests atop an unstable geologic zone, created by the collision of two tectonic plates. Centuries after the Thera eruption, a tsunami generated by an earthquake barreled through the Atlantic, ravaging Lisbon, Portugal. On the morning of November 1, 1755, a major earthquake about 120 miles (200 km) off the coast rocked the capital city. It was All Saint's Day, and worshippers crowded into Lisbon's cathedrals. The earthquake was so strong that it created fissures, or breaks, in the floor of the city. Lisbon's cathedrals collapsed, killing the worshippers, while the candles inside sparked fires that swept through the city.

This illustration depicts Lisbon after a devastating earthquake in 1755 sparked a tragic tsunami that stretched from Norway to North America. Subsequent fires in the Portuguese city spanned five days.

People fled to the harbor to escape the falling buildings but were caught in the tsunami waves. Deep floods swept over the streets and up the Tagus River. Lisbon was destroyed. Even as the water retreated, the fires raged on. By the end of the disaster, an estimated 80,000 to 100,000 people had died. The tsunami also destroyed fishing villages and seaports in Portugal, Spain, and Morocco.

Lisbon took many years to rebuild. The economic cost of tsunamis is high, especially in developed areas. Buildings, roads, bridges, railroads, communications, water, and power systems may be destroyed. More recent, tsunamis have been just as disastrous. On March 28, 1964, tsunamis triggered by a 9.2 magnitude earthquake in Prince William Sound, Alaska, caused 125 deaths and $311 million in property damage. The waves hit the Alaskan coast, including the city of Seward, destroying a chemical truck, overturning ships, washing away railroad bridges, spilling gasoline, and igniting a fire. Eleven people died. Four hours later,

Huge trees were uprooted after a tsunami triggered by an underwater landslide struck Alaska in 1964 and spread death and damage all the way to the coast of Northern California.

the waves crashed onshore at Crescent City, a lumber town on the Northern California coast. Waves as high as 21 feet (6 m) killed eleven people and flattened the business district. A gasoline truck was picked up and flung against electrical wires, sparking a major fire. The cost to the city was more than $7.4 million.

No Means for Survival

In developing countries, a tsunami can destroy people's means of survival, as in Papua New Guinea in 1998. The tropical country with dense mountainous rainforests occupies part of the island of New Guinea in the southwestern Pacific. Its people, representing many indigenous cultures, survive by hunting, gathering, and growing vegetables. Because Papua lies on a major fault line, earthquakes are common. A magnitude 7.1 earthquake struck just after dusk off the island's north coast. Within fifteen minutes, a series of waves as high as 50 feet (15 m) flooded the shores. Thousands were left homeless, and more than 2,000 were drowned.

The 2004 Indian Ocean tsunami impacted developing regions in Indonesia, Thailand, and other South Asian countries. The remote Andanam and Nicobar islands of India were submerged by the waves. After the disaster, the aboriginal tribes living on the islands struggled to survive without safe drinking water, sanitation, shelter, or food. Salt water had polluted their water holes. Rescuers found many people had only coconuts to eat.

Tsunamis also devastate the environment. The waves rip up underwater reefs, destroy fishing grounds and marshes, and sweep away barriers such as sea grass, sand dunes, and mangrove forests. Pouring salt-water over vegetation, the Indian Ocean tsunami destroyed banana, mango, and rice plantations in Sri Lanka. The 1960 tsunami in Chile destroyed valuable farmland. On developed coastlines, industrial pollution is left behind by tsunamis. Spills of hazardous materials such as oil and chemicals destroy plants, water sources, and offshore coral reefs. Sewage collection plants are

Thousands remained missing as this photograph captured the damage from a tsunami off the coast of Papua New Guinea in 1998. The roof of a mission school *(right)* was moved several hundred feet.

also occasionally damaged, dumping wastewater on villages and harbors, and creating environments where people can become sick.

Relief Efforts

Rebuilding after a tsunami is a long process. The Indian Ocean tsunami leveled villages and harbors in more than a dozen countries, costing more than $10 billion in damages. Fuel, water, electricity, and communication systems had to be reconstructed. In Sri Lanka, thousands of fishermen lost their livelihoods. About 80 percent of their fishing grounds were damaged, and nearly 23,000 fishing boats were shattered. International aid organizations donated boats, nets, and money to help people rebuild their lives.

Tsunami survivors must recover their peace of mind, too. Survivors of the Hawaiian tsunamis told their stories in an oral history project by the Pacific Tsunami Museum in Hilo and the University of Hawaii at Manoa. The 1946 tsunami flooded not only Hilo, but also Laupahoehoe Point, a low-lying peninsula. The waves killed twenty-one people there. The survivors still remembered floating at sea, hanging onto logs, and waiting for rescue planes to drop rafts.

Survivors of the Indian Ocean tsunami saw their lives swallowed by water. More than 1,200 children in Thailand lost their parents. Gloria Chen, of the medical relief organization Doctors Without Borders, predicted the tsunami would leave scars on millions. "From our past experience, the people who have undergone such a tragic situation are highly traumatized, as they have lost their dear ones. The mental consequences could last for months and even years," said Chen, in a Voice of America broadcast.

Generous donations to the Indian Ocean tsunami victims flowed in from around the world. Americans alone contributed $1.3 billion to relief efforts. Volunteers poured into South Asia to help with the relief effort. The

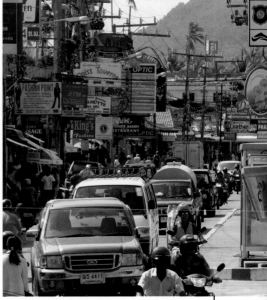

These photographs of Patong, Thailand, compare the impact of the deadly tsunami of 2004 on the left, and its recovery one year later in 2005.

United Nations Children's Fund (UNICEF) opened child development centers in Tamil Nadu, a coastal state in India, to aid the children affected by the tsunami. Staffed by doctors and child workers, the centers provided meals, health care, and counseling.

Surprisingly, large animals sometimes survive a tsunami. In Sri Lanka, more than 22,000 people died in the 2004 tsunami, but elephants, buffalo, and deer survived. According to *National Geographic*, people saw animals acting strangely before the waves hit. Their acute senses may have picked up the earthquake's vibrations, some scientists believe. Other scientists are skeptical, saying there is no proof that animals can predict a tsunami.

Before It's Too Late

At 7:58 AM on December 26, 2004, an earthquake measuring 9.0 on the Richter scale shook the Indian Ocean, the largest earthquake in forty years. Its epicenter was in the Sunda trench, a fault line where two tectonic plates have been colliding for millions of years. One plate was subducting, or pushing beneath the other, building a tremendous strain. That morning, the upper plate snapped back, thrusting the seafloor upward and generating the deadliest tsunami in human history.

Dr. Charles McCreery, a geophysicist in charge of the National Weather Service Pacific Tsunami Warning Center, monitors computers that track earthquake and tsunami activity.

It was 3:07 PM on Christmas Day when scientists at the Pacific Tsunami Warning Center (PTWC) in Hawaii got a seismic signal of a major earthquake near Sumatra in Indonesia. The earthquake appeared to be a magnitude 9.0. Scientists knew that such a huge underwater earthquake could generate a tsunami. The waves would not endanger the Pacific, but they could threaten countries in the Indian Ocean, where there was no tsunami warning system. No one in the region knew they were in danger.

The Hawaiian scientists frantically alerted as many professionals in the region as possible. "We started thinking about who we could call. We talked to the State Department Operations Center and to the military. We called embassies. We talked to the navy in Sri Lanka, any local government official we could get hold of," Barry Hirshorn, a geophysicist at the center, told the *Honolulu Advertiser*.

Without a warning system in place, Hirshorn and his colleagues could not alert enough public safety officials, much less fishermen, villagers, and tourists, in time for everyone to flee to safety.

Path of Destruction

The epicenter of the earthquake was just 155 miles (249 km) off the shore of Sumatra. Within minutes, a tsunami was rolling toward land. The monstrous wave crashed into Banda Aceh, a bustling city on the island's northern tip. Unprepared, hundreds of people were trapped. A massive wall of water swept through the streets, picking up trees, cars, and houses, and pinning people under debris. A second wave soon followed. The water flooded inland up to 1.8 miles (3 km). The city was left in ruins, and the tsunami kept moving through the Indian Ocean. An hour after the earthquake, the waves reached Thailand, flooding the island of Phuket. "If they knew that an earthquake had happened, why didn't they know that there were likely to be these tidal waves, and why didn't they tell Phuket?" asked British tourist Caroline Woods. She told Voice of America that she saw the sky turned to sea, ambulances floating, and people who lost limbs as she tried to escape the waves.

These dramatic before and after aerial photographs show the impact of the tsunami on Banda Aceh province in Indonesia in 2004.

Another hour had passed before the tsunami hit Sri Lanka. A train traveling up the coast of Sri Lanka was derailed by the wave, and most of the passengers drowned. The tsunami kept rolling. Three to four hours later, it slammed into the Maldives, the string of coral islands southwest of Sri Lanka, tearing up buildings and leaving more death in its wake.

The Hawaiian scientists knew the waves could travel as far as the east coast of Africa. This time, they were able to contact government officials. The Kenyan government sprang into action. The Nairobi Foreign Ministry alerted the Kenyan Port Authority and the navy. Television and radio announcers warned people to flee the coast. Boat captains were informed, and police evacuated beaches. The tsunami waves did arrive in Kenya, damaging fishing villages and harbors, but only one fisherman died. The warnings had saved lives.

Warning Systems Around the World

The Indian Ocean tsunami left more than 250,000 people dead, two-thirds of them in Indonesia. An official tsunami warning system could have saved many more lives. Within weeks, world leaders began discussing how to protect the Indian Ocean against future tsunamis. "We cannot stop natural calamities, but we can and must better equip individuals and communities to withstand them," said United Nations Secretary General Kofi Annan. The United Nations Organization for Education, Science, Culture, and Communications (UNESCO) brought together scientists and government leaders to develop a warning system.

Scientists have monitored tsunamis in the Pacific Ocean since the 1940s. The first warning systems were established after the Aleutian Island earthquake of 1946 spawned deadly tsunamis in Alaska and Hawaii. Two years later, the U.S. government established what is now the Pacific Tsunami Warning System. Twenty-six countries belong to the system, which monitors tsunamis in the Pacific. Scientists at the PTWC at Ewa Beach, Hawaii, watch for tsunamis in Hawaii and the Pacific region. The West Coast and Alaska Tsunami Warning Center in Palmer, Alaska, opened after the 1964 Alaskan earthquake and tsunami. Alaskan seismologists and geophysicists monitor both U.S. coasts and the Gulf of Mexico. The centers are overseen by the Honolulu-based International Tsunami Information Center, which coordinates scientific information on tsunamis. All the activities are part of the National Weather Service, a branch of the U.S. National Oceanic and Atmospheric Administration (NOAA). Other countries, including Chile, Japan, and Russia, also have warning centers.

The earliest tsunami warning systems relied on instruments for monitoring earthquakes, tides, and waves. Tide gauges measured changes in tide levels and waves at the shore, while seismometers detected earthquakes. The system was tested in 1952, as a small tsunami headed toward Hawaii. Alerted by the warning system, people fled from the shore. The waves damaged property, but no lives were lost. False alarms were more frequent. In 1986, a false alarm led to the evacuation of Honolulu, costing the state $30 million. Scientists did not have the technology to know if an earthquake had generated a tsunami or not. If a tsunami was underway, they did not know where it was headed.

New Technologies

By 2003, the NOAA started receiving data from a new tsunami warning system able to track waves as they move across the ocean. The Deep-Ocean Assessment and Reporting of Tsunamis system, or DART, measures and reports deep-ocean tsunamis in real time. Tsunameters, which measure water pressure, are anchored to the ocean floor. Even small changes in water pressure can signal a tsunami. The tsunameter sends its information to a buoy on the ocean's surface. The buoy measures surface waves and transmits the information to a satellite, which relays the data to tsunami warning centers. The tsunameters and buoys can be placed far out at sea to detect tsunamis early. The DART system is very accurate.

Back at the warning centers, scientists monitor the DART data for signs of waves. They also look at readings from seismometers and tide gauges in the region. If a tsunami has been generated, scientists are able to immediately track the waves and predict their arrival time on land. Improvements to the first buoy stations ushered in a new system, known as DART II. The United States plans to operate thirty-two DART II buoy stations in the Pacific Ocean and seven in the Atlantic Ocean by 2008.

The buoy in the foreground of this image is connected to sensors on the ocean floor and is a part of the Deep-Ocean Assessment and Reporting of Tsunamis system, or DART.

Within a year of the 2004 tsunami, Indian Ocean nations, with the help of UNESCO, were on their way to a regional tsunami warning system. The system will include more seismometers and tide gauges on shore, as well as deep-sea DART buoys and tsunameters. National tsunami warning centers are also being built. The United States is contributing nearly $17 million to the effort, and U.S. scientists are advising Thailand and other nations on setting up national alert plans. Thailand opened a disaster emergency center and installed beachside alarms. In 2005, Germany helped Indonesia set up two DART buoys in the Indian Ocean. Other countries planned to put DART buoys at the Sunda trench, the site of the tsunami-generating earthquake. In addition, satellites are now being used to track tsunamis in the deep ocean.

Meanwhile, in the Pacific, efforts to improve the tsunami warning system were underway. The PTWC in Hawaii increased its staffing after the Indian Ocean tsunami. By 2006, the center was open twenty-four hours a day, seven days a week. An e-mail system, backed up by an emergency phone tree, was in place to contact Indian Ocean countries. The seismologists and geologists were also trying to issue faster warnings after local earthquakes. The goal was to issue a warning in less than ninety seconds. Today, the world is better prepared than it was in 2004, but detection of a tsunami is just the first step.

Head Inland! 5

Tilly Smith knew something was wrong. The eleven-year-old British girl was vacationing with her family on the island of Phuket, Thailand, during the holidays in 2004. They were enjoying a beautiful day on Maihao Beach. Suddenly, the ocean pulled back from the shore. The water began moving in, rising and bubbling, and foaming with whirlpools. Just two weeks earlier, Tilly had learned about tsunamis in her geography class. When the ocean abruptly receded from the shore, she knew a tsunami might be coming.

Eleven-year-old Tilly Smith reads at a memorial a year after she saved lives by warning people in Phuket, Thailand, that a tsunami was coming because she noticed ocean waters receding.

She screamed for her family to get off the beach. The Smiths ran to the third floor of their hotel. Others on the beach also fled to higher ground. From their safe perch, the Smiths watched three tsunami waves swallow the beach. Not everyone was as fortunate. At a nearby beach, the ocean also seemed to pull back, but since many people ran out to collect fish flopping on bare sand, they were drowned.

Disaster Preparedness

A little knowledge about tsunamis can save lives. Deep-ocean buoys and seismometers help scientists detect a big wave, but the instruments are just a first step in tsunami safety. Communities need to prepare for tsunamis, just like they plan for other disasters. Some of the important pieces of a tsunami readiness plan include warning sirens, evacuation routes, and public shelters. Tsunami education is also very important. The more people know about tsunamis, the better able they are to save themselves.

When a dangerous tsunami is detected in the Pacific Ocean, the Pacific Tsunami Warning Center (PTWC) in Hawaii notifies the countries where the waves are headed. The warnings are received by local governments, which set off sirens and begin evacuation plans. In Japan, television and radio announcers report earthquakes within minutes to give people time to escape a possible tsunami wave. Loudspeakers in coastal towns warn people to evacuate. Tsunamis often hit Japan unexpectedly because many earthquakes occur just off shore, leaving only minutes between the tremors and the big waves. Similarly, an outdoor warning system in San Francisco is set to go off for tsunamis, as well as other disasters.

"Tsunami Alert? Walk, Run, Drive Inland" was the headline of the *Honolulu Advertiser*, the daily newspaper in Hawaii's capital, on January 1, 2005, just days after the Indian Ocean tsunami. Once again, Hawaii was reminding its citizens to be prepared. After two deadly tsunamis in the past century, and many smaller ones, Hawaii has developed one of the world's best tsunami readiness plans, led by the state's Civil Defense department. When a tsunami is detected by the PTWC, the government goes into action. Beachside sirens scream, and announcements go on the air. Tsunami hazard zone signs are visible in low-lying areas. And residents can find evacuation maps in their telephone books.

False Alarm

On May 3, 2006, Hawaii was put to the test after a 7.9 magnitude earthquake shook Tonga, an island group in the South Pacific. The PTWC issued a tsunami warning to Tonga and nearby islands, and put Hawaii under a tsunami advisory. A tsunami advisory, less serious than a warning, means an earthquake has occurred, and that a tsunami is possible but hasn't been spotted yet. People should stay alert. The next alert level, a tsunami watch, indicates that a tsunami could be on its way. People should listen to their radios, television, or Coast Guard emergency frequencies. They should contact family, check emergency supplies, and know their safety routes.

Hawaiian Civil Defense workers at the Diamond Head headquarters activated an emergency operations center and alerted government agencies and the media. Schools in tsunami evacuation zones were closed, and businesses were warned. After tide gauges detected only small waves near the earthquake, and no significant tsunami traveling across the Pacific, the tsunami advisory was cancelled.

If the DART tsunameters and buoys pick up a dangerous tsunami, the PTWC issues a tsunami warning, the highest-level alert. Warnings of a verified tsunami are sent to countries in the waves' path. The warning includes estimated arrival times at different locations.

During a tsunami warning, people should follow tsunami evacuation plans and leave coastal areas immediately. They should never go to the shore to look at a tsunami wave.

If it's not possible to get to higher ground, people should climb to the third story of a building, or even up a tree. During the 1960 tsunami in Chile, many people saved their own lives by climbing trees. One fifteen-year-old boy, Ramón Ramírez, climbed a cypress tree near Maullín, Chile, and watched the water rise beneath him while staying safe. Others survived by grabbing onto floating logs or debris, but that can be dangerous.

Ramón Ramírez stands beside the cypress tree that he climbed to save his life during the 1960 tsunami in Chile.

Preparing ahead of time is important for people in coastal regions with frequent earthquakes. The PTWC recommends that people know the location of shelters and safety routes. At least three days of emergency supplies should be available. Families should also create evacuation plans. Everyone needs to know where to go and how to contact each other. Homeowners should learn how to shut off gas and electricity.

Warning Signs

Many countries at risk of tsunamis still have no warning systems. The earthquake in Tonga in 2006 triggered tsunami alerts across the Pacific, but not in the remote islands, which could not be contacted. Plans to install a warning system in Tonga began soon after. In any case, people need to know tsunami warning signs. First, an earthquake in a coastal area signals a potential tsunami. Water pulling away from the shore is a danger sign. A loud rumbling like a freight train also means a tsunami is coming. When the 1960 Chilean earthquake sent a tsunami to Japan, a fireman was on early-morning watch at the harbor of Onagawa. Kimura Kunio noticed that the water looked unusual, and he awoke the townspeople, who safely fled to higher ground. Tsunamis that are generated by local earthquakes, volcanoes, or landslides do not give people much time to evacuate. Sometimes only minutes separate the earthquake and tsunami. The Papua New Guinea tsunami on July 17, 1998, hit land minutes after an earthquake struck just 20 miles (32 km) from shore.

Some people ignore all warnings and try to see a tsunami, but if the wave is visible, it is impossible to outrun it. On October 4, 1994, hundreds of surfers rushed to beaches along the North Shore of the Hawaiian island of Oahu. The state had issued a tsunami warning after an earthquake struck near Japan. The surfers were hoping to catch a big wave. Traffic clogged coastal roads as people hurried to escape. A few others drove toward beaches. Fortunately, the small tsunami was not observable on Oahu. If it had been a big one, the people would have risked their lives. After a tsunami, people should stay away from flooded areas. The water can be contaminated by dumped chemicals, or electrically charged from downed power lines. People should also avoid floating debris, which can smash against them and overturn rescue boats. Even after the waves pull back, flash floods can create new hazards.

"Move to Higher Ground!"

As tsunami awareness grows, coastal communities are better prepared. At 10:56 PM on June 14, 2005, a tsunami bulletin went out from the West Coast and Alaska Tsunami Warning Center. A 7.2 magnitude earthquake was detected off Northern California. The

At 10:56 PM on June 14, 2005, a tsunami bulletin went out from the West Coast and Alaska Tsunami Warning Center. A 7.2 magnitude earthquake was detected off Northern California.

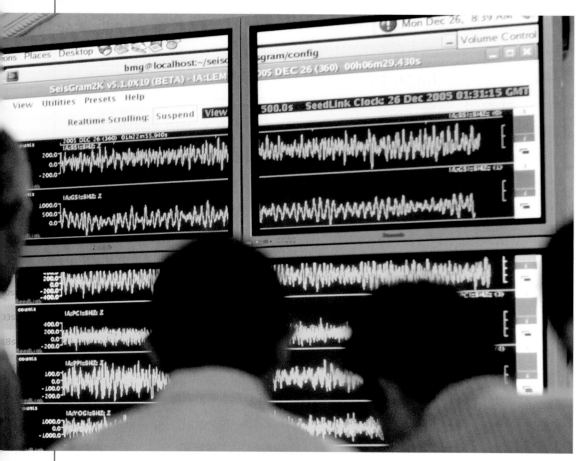

Indonesian meteorologists check a seismograph screen in 2005 during a simulated demonstration of the tsunami early-warning system in Jakarta a year after a deadly tsunami there killed thousands.

entire West Coast was at risk of a tsunami, the warning stated. "It is not known—repeat not known—if a tsunami exists, but a tsunami may have been generated," the bulletin stated. "Therefore, persons in low-lying coastal areas should be alert to instructions from their local emergency officials. Persons on the beach should move to higher ground . . . "

Local officials took the warning seriously in Crescent City, a seaside California community near the Oregon border. People hadn't forgotten the tsunami of 1964. Triggered by the Alaskan earthquake, the 20-foot (6 m) waves killed eleven people, flooded buildings, ignited fires, and swept away houses, lumber, and even a bridge. Crescent City had been testing its tsunami alarm system every month. That night in 2005, the alarm wasn't a test. When it went off, people jumped in their cars and drove to higher ground. The earthquake did not create a tsunami, but people felt secure knowing they had been warned.

TsunamiReady

Coastal communities are getting help from TsunamiReady, a program of the NOAA's National Weather Service. A TsunamiReady community must have a twenty-four-hour warning and emergency operations center, and a weather-monitoring system. The community holds public meetings, trains people to spot tsunamis, and organizes emergency drills. When a city has a plan in place, the National Weather Service certifies it as "TsunamiReady." The Quinault Indian Nation on the Olympic Peninsula of Washington is the first Native American tribe to become a TsunamiReady community. The tribal population resides at the mouth of the

Quinault River. According to tribal legend, and now scientific fact, a major tsunami on January 26, 1700, inundated their land. The tsunami was caused by an earthquake in the Cascadia subduction zone, the 680-mile (1,094 km) fault 50 miles (80 km) off the coast from southern Canada to Northern California. A similar earthquake and tsunami could occur at any time. By May 2006, twenty-nine communities in Florida, Virginia, Alaska, Hawaii, California, Oregon, Washington, and Puerto Rico were TsunamiReady.

The 2004 tsunami spurred Indian Ocean countries to establish tsunami safety procedures, but protecting people in remote islands and villages is difficult. Unlike in California or Oregon, people in these countries might not have access to radio, television, or the Internet. Installing and maintaining tsunami sirens is expensive. A city on Sumatra tested its new tsunami early-warning system in December 2005. The test began when the mayor of Padang, the capital of the province of West Sumatra, received a false report of an earthquake from Indonesia's Meteorological Agency. When the sirens blew, some 5,000 people evacuated to higher ground. The drill was a success. People were now confident that they could escape a tsunami.

Wave Labs and Mangrove Forests

6

S hocked at the devastation caused by the Indian Ocean tsunami, the world looked to scientists for answers. Research into tsunamis had lagged behind the study of other natural disasters. Since major tsunamis happen rarely, studying the waves was not a priority for institutions. That changed when the world saw the wide-scale destruction caused by the giant waves.

Searching for Answers

Starting in 2005, the U.S. Congress increased funding

to the NOAA to improve the nation's tsunami warning system. In the two years since the Indian Ocean catastrophe, the NOAA, which is the agency responsible for tsunami research and safety, received more than $28 million in extra funding. "All facets of NOAA's tsunami program—from research to operations—have been expanded. The result is a nation more prepared to act should a tsunami threaten our shores," said Conrad C. Lautenbacher, the retired navy vice admiral who led the NOAA in 2006. More buoys were placed in the ocean, and more research got underway. Geophysicists, engineers, and mathematicians with an interest in tsunamis got very busy. An exciting new chapter in tsunami research unfolded, with one simple goal: saving lives.

Better Forecasting Tools

In the past, tsunamis were unpredictable, but scientists are beginning to forecast their impact on a particular coast. In Seattle, after the 2004 tsunami, a fresh group of mathematicians and software engineers was hired at the National Center for Tsunami Research, a part of the NOAA's Pacific Marine Environmental Laboratory. They went to work building computer models to forecast tsunamis. Using data about the earthquake, seafloor, coastline, and wave patterns of tsunamis, the Seattle researchers created forecasting models that include information on earthquakes and whether they will trigger tsunamis; the size and speed of the waves; and the impact on land. Scientists now know that earthquakes under 7.0 are less likely to trigger tsunamis and that tsunamis grow larger in shallow shorelines.

Mathematicians contribute their knowledge to tsunami modeling. They use wave equations to describe and plot ocean waves. A Canadian mathematical analyst is using calculations to help predict tsunami wave patterns and height. Walter Craig, a professor at McMaster

Conrad C. Lautenbacher *(left)*, administrator of the National Oceanic and Atmospheric Administration (NOAA), speaks with John H. Marburger III, science advisor to President Bush, about expanding U.S. tsunami warning capabilities in 2005.

University in Ontario, studies the motions of waves by using computer models. Calculating the size and patterns of waves is important for tsunami research. Using wave equations and seafloor maps, mathematicians can predict the size and arrival time of a tsunami. Using this information, the National Center for Tsunami Research is developing a more accurate tsunami forecasting system.

To help protect people, scientists at NOAA's National Tsunami Hazard Mitigation Program are developing impact maps of coastal communities to pinpoint regions at risk. They study the paths of recent floods and check for geologic evidence of past tsunamis. Low coastal land is identified. The scientists then draw maps showing areas at risk. Safety officials use the maps to develop tsunami evacuation plans and decide on future land development.

Scientists also learn from creating their own tsunami waves. At a wave research laboratory at Oregon State University, they use a state-of-the-art tsunami wave basin to build wave models to study their effects on coastlines. One recent experiment by Dr. Philip Liu, a professor at Cornell University, focused on tsunamis caused by landslides. Researchers slid a rectangular box down a slope into the wave tank. Using electronic and video sensors, they measured the waves and the run-up, or how far the waves traveled over land. Experiments like this one help scientists understand tsunamis.

Research at the Site

Field research is important. In the wake of a major tsunami, scientists and engineers rush to the scene to gather information. Shortly after the tsunami in Papua New Guinea, the International Tsunami Survey Team brought instruments to measure the water levels and seismographs and other tools to document the event. They recorded the damage to buildings, noted the highest

The Tsunami Wave Basin is a part of the Hinsdale Wave Research Laboratory at Oregon State University, a facility to help scientists understand the impact and force of tsunami waves.

level of water on trees and buildings, and interviewed eye-witnesses. The scientists also collected soil samples. Their observations helped them prepare for the next tsunami.

In fact, sediment left by tsunamis holds clues on the height of the waves and their impact on land. Soil also tells the stories of historic tsunamis. Geologist Brian Atwater of the U.S. Geological Survey discovered layers of dark-gray sand stacked between slabs of brownish soil along the Niawiakum River in Washington state. He believed tsunamis had picked up sand next to the shore and dumped it inland. The thickest sand layer was determined to match the date of a tsunami in Japan on January 26, 1700. No written record of this tsunami existed in the United States, though the Quinault Indian Nation has legends of the event. Since no earthquake was felt in Japan at the time, the tsunami must have been caused by a distant event. The geological evidence on the Niawiakum River supported the theory that a massive earthquake occurred in 1700 in the Cascadia subduction zone. This is the long fault off the coast of the Pacific Northwest, which probably triggered the tsunamis in Washington state and Japan.

Learning from the Past

Meanwhile, countries are looking at practical ways to manage their coasts. Hilo did not rebuild many of its harbor businesses after the 1964 tsunami; instead, public parks along the seafront offer a natural shield to private property. Japan has worked to protect its coastlines, as it did on Okushiri Island after the July 12, 1993, tsunami. A 7.8 magnitude earthquake shook Okushiri that night, and within minutes, a tsunami approached the island. Waves as high as 95 feet (29 m) flooded the island. Some 200 people died in the earthquake and tsunami, which destroyed houses, fishing boats, and port facilities. To shield Okushiri from tsunamis, Japan built a concrete seawall around parts of the island. The wall has six gates, shut by safety officers during a tsunami emergency. New houses were constructed on piles of landfill to avoid flood damage. Every home on Okushiri has an alarm to warn residents of earthquakes and tsunamis. Solar-powered evacuation signs light up the roads at night. Where a village was swept away in 1993, Okushiri built a memorial park. No buildings are allowed there.

An Indian family mourns those lost in the devastating tsunami that struck Tamil Nadu in 2004. The region's forest department has planted trees along the beach to help protect it from future waves.

A tsunami warning tower rises above tourists in Patong Beach in the southern Phuket province of Thailand in 2005, one year after a deadly tsunami claimed 5,400 lives there.

Coastal forests and vegetation can break the waves and slow flooding, as well as block debris that causes injuries. In many tropical countries, mangrove forests grow on coastlines. In recent years, the mangroves in Asia have been cut down for hotels, shrimp farms, and other economic projects, but during the Indian Ocean tsunami, coasts with mangroves sustained less damage. Fearing future tsunamis, several countries have pledged to restore their mangrove forests. One day in 2005, villagers in Kajhu, on Sumatra, gathered on the beach with buckets filled with mangrove and pine seedlings. They dug trenches and planted the seedlings at the edge of the water. The planting project is one of many efforts across the Indian Ocean to shore up the coast.

Risk Assessment

One question remains: Will a major tsunami impact the United States? Tsunami researchers say that it is likely.

California has experienced dozens of tsunamis in the past 200 years. Most were not destructive, but researchers believe there is the possibility of a near-shore earthquake or landslide that could cause flooding levels of 40 feet (13 m) on the heavily populated California coast. Oregon and Washington are also at risk if a major earthquake occurs in the Cascadia subduction zone, as it did in 1700. Across the continent, tsunamis generated by an earthquake or volcano in the Atlantic or Caribbean could threaten New York City. Scientists are watching the Cumbre Vieja volcano in Spain's Canary Islands. If the volcano erupts, it could trigger a massive landslide fueling an Atlantic tsunami powerful enough to reach the United States.

With the new tsunami detection technology, the world is better prepared than it was in 2004. Meanwhile, the best defense against tsunamis is good planning. One weekend in April 2005, a siren blew in Seaside, Oregon, a small resort town that sits at sea level on the Pacific Ocean. The residents of Seaside dropped what they were doing and began walking and bicycling uphill away from the coast. Rather than panicking at the prospect of a big wave flooding their town, the people knew to get to higher ground. This time, the siren was a test, but if a tsunami ever hits Seaside, the town is ready.

Glossary

bore A traveling wave with a wall of water.

epicenter The point on the earth's surface right above the focus of an earthquake.

fault A break in the earth's crust that shows movement.

leading depression wave A tsunami wave that leads with a trough, drawing water back from the shore.

magnitude The amount of energy released by an earthquake, usually measured by the Richter scale.

run-up The maximum height of the tsunami onshore above normal sea level.

seismograph An instrument that records the vibrations during an earthquake.

subduction zone An area where the crust of the ocean floor dives beneath the edge of the lighter continental crust and sinks down into the earth's mantle.

tectonic plate A piece of the earth's crust, either oceanic or continental.

thrust fault An earthquake caused by a slip along a sloping fault where the rock above the fault is pushed upwards.

trough The lowest point of a wave.

wave height The distance from the wave trough to the crest.

wave length The distance from one crest to the next.

For More Information

International Tsunami Information Center
737 Bishop Street, Mauka Tower, Suite 2200
Honolulu, HI 96813
(808) 532-6423
Web site: http://www.tsunamiwave.info

Pacific Marine Environmental Laboratory
7600 Sand Point Way NE
Seattle, WA 98115
(206) 526-6239
Web site: http://www.pmel.noaa.gov

Pacific Tsunami Warning Center (PTWC)
91-270 Fort Weaver Road
Ewa Beach, HI 96706-2928
(808) 689-8207
Web site: http://www.prh.noaa.gov/ptwc

Web Sites

Due to the changing nature of Internet links, Rosen
Publishing has developed an online list of Web sites
related to the subject of this book. This site is updated
regularly. Please use this link to access the list:

http://www.rosenlinks.com/in/tsun

For Further Reading

Kehret, Peg. *Escaping the Giant Wave*. New York, NY: Aladdin, 2004.

Stewart, Gail. *Catastrophe in Southern Asia: The Tsunami of 2004*. San Diego, CA: Lucent Books, 2005.

Thompson, Luke. *The Tsunami Man*. Honolulu, HI: University of Hawaii Press, 2002.

Vogel, Carole Garbuny. *Shifting Shores*. New York, NY: Scholastic Library, 2003.

Bibliography

Atwater, Brian F., et al. "Surviving a Tsunami—Lessons from Chile, Hawaii, and Japan." U.S. Geological Survey. Retrieved May 20, 2006 (http://pubs.usgs.gov/circ/c1187).

Brand, David. "Limiting Tsunami Damage Is Possible with Coastal Management and Zoning Policies." *Cornell News*. Retrieved May 20, 2006 (http:// www.news.cornell.edu/releases/July98/Liu.tsunami.deb.html).

Dudley, Walter C., and Min Lee. *Tsunami!* Honolulu, HI: University of Hawaii Press, 1998.

Flynn, Ray, and Kyle Fletcher, et al. "The Cascadia Subduction Zone." The Pacific Northwest Seismograph Network. Retrieved May 20, 2006 (http://www. geophys.washington.edu/SEIS/PNSN/HAZARDS/ CASCADIA/cascadia_zone.html).

Geist, Eric L. "Life of a Tsunami." U.S. Geological Service. Retrieved May 20, 2006 (http://walrus.wr. usgs.gov/tsunami/basics.html).

Heuer, Kapua, et al. "Tsunamis Remembered." Center for Oral History, University of Hawaii at Manoa. Retrieved May 20, 2006 (http://www.oralhistory. hawaii.edu/pages/historical/tsunami.html).

Hogen, Jenny, and Emma Young. "Tsunami: Will We Be Ready for the Next One?" Newscientist.com. Retrieved May 20, 2006 (http://www.newscientist. com/channel/earth/tsunami/mg18524825.000- tsunami-will-we-be-ready-for-the-next-one.html).

"How Kenya, Seyechelles Avoided Tsunami Disaster." Afrol News. Retrieved May 20, 2006 (http:// www.afrol.com/articles/15120).

Jaffe, Bruce, and Guy Gelfenbaum. "Preliminary Analysis of Sedimentary Deposits from the 1998 Papua New Guinea Tsunami." U.S. Geological Service. Retrieved May 20, 2006 (http://walrus.wr. usgs.gov/tsunami/itst.html#results).

Janin, Jennifer. "Indian Ocean Tsunami: A Remembrance." Voice of America. Retrieved May 20, 2006 (http://

www.voanews.com/english/archive/2005-12/ 2005-12-23-voa24.cfm).

"Modeling and Forecasting." NOAA National Center for Tsunami Research. Retrieved May 20, 2006 (http:// nctr.pmel.noaa.gov/ research.html).

Myles, Douglas. *The Great Waves*. New York, NY: McGraw-Hill, 1985.

Onishi, Norimitsu. "Japanese Isle Debates Their Value." *Seoul Times*. Retrieved May 20, 2006 (http:// theseoultimes.com/ST/?url=/ST/db/read.php?idx=1540).

Prager, Ellen J., et al. *Furious Earth: The Science and Nature of Earthquakes, Volcanoes, and Tsunamis*. New York, NY: McGraw-Hill, 2000.

"South Asia Earthquakes and Tsunamis." World Health Organization. Retrieved May 20, 2006 (http://www. who.int/hac/crises/international/asia_tsunami/en).

"Tsunami Family Saved by Schoolgirl's Geography Lesson." *National Geographic News*. Retrieved May 20, 2006 (http://news.nationalgeographic.com/ news/2005/01/0118_050118_tsunami_geography_ lesson_2.html).

Walter, Craig, "The Math of Deadly Waves." Retrieved May 20, 2006 (http://www.eurekalert.org/pub_releases/ 2006-02/nsae-tmo021706.php).

Winchester, Simon. *Krakatoa: The Day the World Exploded: August 27, 1883*. New York, NY: Harper Collins, 2005.

Index

About the Author

Ann Malaspina specializes in writing books for young readers about history, science, and geography. She lives in New Jersey.

Photo Credits

Cover: (top left) © Jordon R. Beesley/US Navy/Getty Images, (top right) © Emmanuel Dunand/AFP/Getty Images, (bottom) © AFP/Getty Images; pp. 3 (left), 29, 40, 56 © Saeed Khan/AFP/Getty Images; pp. 3 (right), 21 (top) © STR/AFP/Getty Images; p. 4 (top) © Kazuhiro Nogi/AFP/Getty Images; p. 4 (middle) © Sena Vidanagama/AFP/Getty Images; p. 4 (bottom) © Paula Bronstein/Getty Images; p. 6 © AFP/Getty Images; pp. 8, 10, 17, 27, 49 © AP/Wide World Photos; p. 11 (top, bottom) © Choo Youn-Kong/AFP/Getty Images; p. 11 (middle) © Jewel Samad/AFP/Getty Images; p. 13 © Pacific Tsunami Museum—Beago Collection; p. 15 © Corbis; p. 21 (middle, bottom) © AFP/Joel Saget (top) Samad/Getty Images; p. 23 © NASA/GSFC/MITI/ERSDAC/JAROS, and U.S./Japan ASTER Science Team; p. 24 © Lisbon City Museum/handout/Reuters/Corbis; p. 25 © USGS; p. 30 (top) © Scott Barbour/Getty Images, Inc.; p. 30 (middle, bottom) © Earth Observatory/NASA/GSFC; p. 31 © Marco Garcia/Getty Images; p. 33 © DigitalGlobe/Getty Images; p. 37 Marie Eble/NOAA/PMEL; p. 39 (top) © Farid/AFP/Getty Images; pp. 39 (middle), 49 (top) © Pornchai Kittiwongsakul/AFP/Getty Images; pp. 39 (bottom), 43 USGS Circular 1187; p. 46 © Adek Berry/AFP/Getty Images; p. 49 (bottom) © Frederic J. Brown/AFP/Getty Images; p. 51 © Matthew Cavanaugh/Getty Images; p. 53 O. H. Hinsdale Wave Research Laboratory; p. 55 © Sebastuab D'Souza/AFP/Getty Images.

Designer: Tom Forget; Editor: Joann Jovinelly; Photo Researcher: Amy Feinberg